Monographic Journals of the Near East *Afroasiatic Linguistics* 7/2 (December 1979)

LOVE THROUGH DEATH IN MODERN HEBREW
A SYNTACTIC TREATMENT

by

Zafrira Malisdorf

Ben Gurion University of the Negev, Israel

Investigating the verb *la-mut* 'to die' in Hebrew, one observes that, depending on the context, it has a secondary meaning ranging from 'want' to 'love'. It will be argued here that the different readings of the verb stem from a regularity in Hebrew according to which some verbs may change their interpretation in a predictable way, depending on their syntactic environment; when followed by a NP, the verb is interpreted as a comment on a situation; where followed by S, no such comment is required. The syntactic arguments for the analysis are based upon the operation of the Noun Phrase Constraint. The semantic arguments assume that a sentence embedded in a NP is a presupposition of the entire sentence. This analysis suggests that some verbs of perception and the like have as one of their semantic features [± comment], and some may add such a feature through the process of the semantic reading of the entire utterance.

Table of Contents

In colloquial Hebrew one can find sentences (1-4) where the verb *la-mut*'to die' is used to convey the meanings 'want very much' and 'love', which are different from the basic meaning of *la-mut.*

(1)	*ani*	*meta*	*še-yatxilu*	*kvar*	*tiyulim*	*le-kahir*
	I	dying	that-will-begin	already	trips	to-Cairo

'I would very much like to see that trips to Cairo would already begin'

(2)	*ani*	*meta*	*al*	*ha-sefer*	*ha-ze*
	I	dying	about	the-book	the-this

'I am crazy about this book'

(3)	*ani*	*meta*	*al*	*ha-raayon*	*še-nisa*	*le-kahir*
	I	dying	about	the-idea	that-we-will-travel	to-Cairo

'I am crazy about the idea that we will travel to Cairo'

(4)	*ani*	*meta*	*al*	*ha-raayon*	*še-hicata*
	I	dying	about	the-idea	that-you-proposed

'I am crazy about the idea that you have proposed'

In this paper it will be argued that some of the features which allow for the various readings of the verb *la-mut* 'to die' follow from a regularity that exists in Hebrew and is therefore predictable. It particular I will argue that it is the presence or absence of a NP following the verb which determines whether the reading of the verb should be 'want to very much' on the one hand or 'love' on the other. The analysis required to explain the above will provide a subcategorization for a group of verbs in the language. In addition, the fact that a syntactic theoretical construct has a crucial role in determining the meaning of an utterance provides further support for the postulation of a grammatical system in a description of a language.

The discussion will center around embedded sentences in object position only and the argument will be presented in the following way.

In Section 2 I will discuss two classes of verbs:

(a) Verbs which do not change their meaning and where the V is followed by an S not dominated by a NP;
(b) Verbs which do not change their meaning regardless of whether the V is followed on the surface by a NP or an S.

In both cases syntactic evidence drawn from the interaction of movement rules with the Noun Phrase Constraint (NPC) will be presented to support the following arguments:

In (a) the S can under no circumstances be analyzed as being dominated by a NP.
In (b), despite the different surface sequences, all of them have to be analyzed as being dominated by a NP.

Section 3 will be concerned with verbs that do change their meaning depending on the context in which they occur. For example:

(5) a. *hitrašamti* *še-hem* *higiu* *ba-zman*
had-the-impression-I that-they arrived on-time
'I had the impression that they had arrived on time'

b. *hitrašamti* *mi-ze* *še-hem* *higiu* *ba-zman*
had-the-impression-I from-that that-they arrived on-time
'I was impressed by their arriving on time'

These verbs, it will be argued, have to be subcategorized in the lexicon as allowing both a NP and an S node to follow them. In Section 4 an attempt will be made to provide a semantic explanation for the phenomenon discussed. This explanation will be concerned with both the features of the verbs and the semantic content of the node NP. The conclusion will involve an explanation of sentences (1-4). The general framework in which the analysis is performed is that of transformational generative grammar. In addition I am assuming the existence of the following rules and constraints in Hebrew, the operation of which has been argued for in Malisdorf (1975).

(i) Prepositional Phrase Preposing (PPP)[1]

	X	PP	Y	
SD:	1	2	3	⟹ Optional
SC:	2 1	∅	3	

Examples:

(6) *Dan kana* *et* *ha-sefer*
Dan bought OM the-book (OM=Object Marker)

(7) *et* *ha-sefer* *Dan kana*
OM the-book Dan bought

(ii) *Lo* (= Neg.) - Movement Rule (LMR)[2]

---

[1]Prepositional Phrase Preposing (PPP) is a rule which combines Topicalization and Question Formation as they appear in Chayen and Dror (1975: 113, 146 respectively). PPP is assumed here for the purpose of explaining the syntactic behavior of sentences dominated by a NP as opposed to sentences which are not. Given the above, I have ignored various problems which this rule presents (and which are mentioned in Malisdorf 1975: Chapter 2, n.9.1). For a more extensive discussion of the preposing of elements in a sentence see Ben Horin (1976).

[2]The arguments for *lo*-Movement Rule (LMR) are found in Malisdorf (1975: 11-28). However it should be noted here that LMR is not the same rule as Neg. Transportation (or Neg. Raising) discussed extensively by Klima (1967: 319-320), Jackendorff (1972: 254), Lakoff (1971) and others. The framework in which LMR was postulated is one which adheres to the Meaning Preserving Hypothesis proposed by Katz and Postal (1964). As a result LMR moves only the negation element *lo* 'not'

	X	V	Y	*lo*	Z
SD:	1	2	3	4	5 ⟹ Optional
SC:	1 4	2	3	∅	5

Examples:

(8) *moše ohev* ***lo*** *et rut* ***ki-im*** *et dina*
Moses loves **not** OM Ruth **but** OM Dina

(9) *moše lo ohev et rut ki-im et dina*
Moses not loves OM Ruth but OM Dina

(iii) The Noun Phrase Constraint (NPC) which states that "No element can move out of a sentence embedded in a NP":

Examples:

(10) *dan sameax al* $[_{NP}$ *ze* $[_{S}$ *še-rut nas'a le-tel-aviv*]
Dan happy about it that-Ruth travelled to-Tel-Aviv

(11) **le-tel-aviv dan sameax al* $[_{NP}$ *ze* $[_{S}$ *še-rut nas'a*]
to-Tel-Aviv Dan happy about it that-Ruth travelled

The NPC, it should be noted, is different from the Complex Noun Phrase Constraint of Ross (1967: 70) since it restricts the application of movement rules even in cases where the head NP is [−lexical].

2. Single-meaning Verbs

2.1 *Syntactic arguments for Phrase Structure Rule: Verb Phrase → Verb + Sentence*
Consider the following sentences:

(12) *dan mešaer še-ha-šalom yavo be-karov*
Dan supposes that-the-peace will-come in-near
'Dan assumes that peace will soon come'

(13) **dan mešaer et ze še-ha-salom yavo be-karov*
Dan supposes OM it that-the-peace will-come in-near

when it is part of the constitutent *lo...ki-im* 'not but', and where the scope of *lo* is not changed. Given the meaning preserving hypotheses, this rule cannot apply to any Negation element if there is a change in its scope and therefore it does not apply in the cases for which Negative Transportation has been postulated.

(14) **dan mešaer et še-ha-šalom yavo be-karov*
Dan supposes OM that-the-peace will-come in-near

The surface sequence of the elements in (12-14) is (15) a-c respectively:

(15) a. NP + V + S

b. NP + V + Prep. + N + S

c. NP + V + Prep. + S

The ungrammaticality of (13) and (14) occurs in structures which either contain a NP before the embedded S (13) or include a Prep. before the S indicating the presence of such a NP node (14). Given that this is the case there is no reason to postulate a NP exhaustively dominating the embedded S in the examples above.

Further support for the above claim comes from the syntactic behavior of structures such as (13-14) which allow T-rules to move elements out of their embedded S's, i.e. the NPC is inapplicable.

In (16) LMR has applied to an element in the embedded S generating a grammatical sentence (b).

In (17) PPP has applied to an element in the embedded S again generating a grammatical sentence (b).

(16) a. *moše maniax* [$_S$ *še-**lo** yihye šalom ki-im milxama*]
Moses assumes that-**not** will-be peace but war

b. *moše **lo** maniax* [$_S$ *še-yihye šalom ki-im milxama*]
Moses **not** assumes that-will be peace but war

(17) a. *yael svura* [$_S$ *še-yihye šalom **ba-ezor***]
Yael is-of-the-opinion that-will be peace **in-the-area**

b. ***ba-ezor** yael svura* [$_S$ *še-yihye šalom*]
in-the-area Yael is-of-the-opinion that-will-be peace

2.2 *Syntactic arguments for Phrase Structure Rule: Noun Phrase → (Noun Phrase) + Sentence*
Consider now the following sentences:

(18) a. *dan sameax **še-saadat** higia be-šalom*
Dan happy **that**-Sadat arrived in-peace
'Dan is happy that Sadat has safely arrived'

b. *dan sameax **al** še-saadat higia be-šalom*
Dan happy **about that**-Sadat arrived in-peace
'Dan is happy that Sadat has safely arrived'

c. *dan sameax* ***al*** *ze še-saadat higia be-šalom*
Dan happy **about it that**-Sadat arrived in-peace
'Dan is happy that Sadat has safely arrived'

(19) a. *raxel mezuazat še-ha-rofim šovtim*
Rachel shocked **that**-the-doctors strike
'Rachel is shocked that the doctors are striking'

b. *raxel mezuazat* ***al*** *še-ha-rofim šovtim*
Rachel shocked **about that**-the-doctors strike
'Rachel is shocked that the doctors are striking'

c. *raxel mezuazat* ***mi-ze*** *še-ha-rofim šovtim*
Rachel shocked **from-it that**-the-doctors strike
'Rachel is shocked that the doctors are striking'

(20) a. *yaakov meruce še-ha-švita nimšexet*
Jacob satisfied **that**-the-strike continues
'Jacob is satisfied that the strike continues'

b. *yaakov meruce* ***al*** *še-ha-švita nimšexet*
Jacob satisfied **about that**-the-strike continues
'Jacob is satisfied that the strike continues'

c. *yaakov meruce* ***mi-ze*** *še-ha-švita nimšexet*
Jacob satisfied **from-it that**-the-strike continues
'Jacob is satisfied that the strike continues'

The surface sequence of the elements in (18-20) a-c is (21) a-c respectively:

(21) a. NP + V + S[3]

b. NP + V + Prep. + S

c. NP + V + Prep. + N + S

In other words, on the surface, the only embedded S most appropriately analyzed as dominated by a NP is the one in (21) c where the S is preceded by a demonstrative N. Nonetheless the meaning of the verb does not change in the way suggested in the introduction. For the argument to hold, it is therefore necessary to show that all the embedded S's in (21) are dominated by a NP which is the reason for their shared meaning. Examples (22-24) provide evidence for the embedded S's in (21) a, b being dominated by a NP. The demonstration is based on the application of LMR and PPP to elements in the embedded S moving them outside the domain of that S. Both of these rules are movement rules and are thus constrained by the NPC.

[3]See Rosenbaum (1967) for further arguments in favor of expanding VP as V-S in some cases of complementation.

(22) a. *ani mictaer* [$_{PP}$ *al* [$_{NP}$ *ze* [$_{S}$ *še-hu lo roce šalom ki-im rak milxama*]]]
I sorry about it that-he not want peace but only war

b. **ani lo mictaer* [$_{PP}$ *al* [$_{NP}$ *ze* [$_{S}$ *še-hu roce šalom ki-im rak milxama*]]]
I **not** sorry about it that-he wants peace but only war

(23) a. *ani mictaer* [$_{PP}$ *al* [$_{S}$ *še-hu lo roce šalom ki-im rak milxama*]]
I sorry about that-he not want peace but only war

b. **ani* **lo** *mictaer* [$_{PP}$ *al* [$_{S}$ *še-hu roce šalom ki-im rak milxama*]]
I **not** sorry about that-he wants peace but only war

(24) a. *ani mictaer* [$_{S}$ *še-hu lo roce šalom ki-im milxama*]
I sorry that-he not want peace but only war

b. **ani* **lo** *mictaer* [$_{S}$ *še-hu roce šalom ki-im rak milxama*]
I **not** sorry that-he wants peace but only war

(22) is derived by applying LMR to the derived structure (25). (The deep structure I believe is slightly different, cf. Malisdorf (1975: ch.2.))

(25)

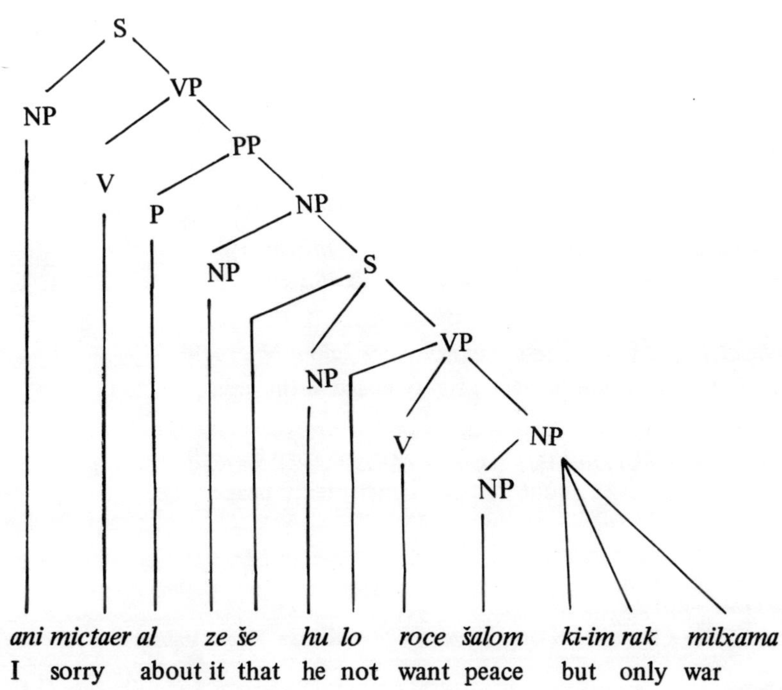

lo, which is the element permuted by the LMR, is dominated by a NP. The ungrammaticality of (22) b is due to the fact that the application of LMR violates the NPC.

In examples (23) and (24) there is no surface NP which can readily justify embedding the S in a NP. However, given that the syntactic behavior and the meaning of (23) and (24) are similar to that of (22), it is plausible to assume that their underlying structure is (25), where the S is exhaustively dominated by a NP. This behavior, as will be demonstrated in Section 3, is not shared by S's immediately following verbs and which cannot be preceded by either a Prep. or a Prep. + *ze* 'this'.

Further justification for having a NP exhaustively dominating an S concerns the expansion of a PP node in Hebrew. Not assuming $[_{NP}$ S] makes it necessary to postulate (26) a for Hebrew, in addition to having (26) b.

(26) a. PP → P + S

b. PP → P + NP

Allowing two different expansions of PP may unnecessarily complicate the grammar, creating a situation where constraints on movement rules have to be stated separately for NP's following Prep. and S's which follow a Prep.[4]

The last argument in favor of the above analysis of (23) and (24) stems from the fact that in (22-24) the embedded S expresses a proposition which has truth value. Not relating the first three examples to one particular structure, be it the structure of the S or the structure of the verb itself[5], renders the similarity between these embedded S's accidental.

Examples (27-29) are further illustrations of the similarity between structures such as (21). In these examples the PPP rule has applied to elements in the embedded S. Again the ungrammaticality of all the b sentences can be accounted for if the S is dominated by a NP and the NPC has been violated.

(27) a. *rut mezuazat* $[_{PP}$ *mi-* $[_{NP}$ *ze* $[_{S}$ *še-tifroc milxama* ***ba-ezor***]]]
Ruth shocked from-it that-will-break-out war **in-the-area**

b. ***ba-ezor** *rut mezuazat* $[_{PP}$ *mi-* $[_{NP}$ *ze* $[_{S}$ *še-tifroc milxama*]]]
In-the-area Ruth shocked from-it that-will-break-out war

(28) a. *rut mezuazat* $[_{PP}$ *al* $[_{NP}$ $[_{S}$ *še-lo nextam xoze šalom* ***ba-ezor***]]]
Ruth shocked about that-not signed treaty peace **in-the-area**

b. ***ba-ezor** *rut mezuazat* $[_{PP}$ *al* $[_{NP}$ $[_{S}$ *še-lo nextam xoze šalom*]]]
In-the-area Ruth shocked about that-not signed treaty peace

[4]For arguments against postulating a NP which is later deleted in cases such as 26, see Malisdorf (1975:2.7).

[5]The examples thus far are similar to the ones with factive verbs described by Kiparsky and Kiparsky (1971). It is in their sense that the notion of a presupposition is used here.

(29) a. *rut mezuazat* [$_{NP}$ [$_{S}$ *še-lo nextam xoze šalom* ***ba-ezor***]]
Ruth shocked that-not signed treaty peace **in-the-area**

b. ****ba-ezor*** *rut mezuazat* [$_{NP}$ [$_{S}$ *še-lo nextam xoze šalom*]]
In-the-area Ruth shocked that-not signed treaty peace

I have so far discussed two classes of verbs in Hebrew. The first class includes verbs which cannot be followed by a NP but which must be followed by an S. These verbs retain the same meaning in all contexts. The second class includes verbs which when followed by an embedded S also retain their meaning whether the S is preceded by a Prep. + N, a Prep., or $\emptyset$. The embedded S's in these cases behave syntactically in a similar way, i.e. all of them are subject to the NPC, and therefore it is assumed that the S in these cases is dominated by a NP.

We now turn to the cases where the verb can be followed by either a NP or an S and where changes in meaning do occur.

3. Multiple-meaning Verbs

3.1 *The various readings of* le-ha'arix *and their syntactic correlates*
Sentences (30-31) involve the verb *le-ha'arix*, whose meaning in the context is either 'to appreciate' or 'to estimate'.

In (30) the verb is followed by an S and in (31) it is followed by a PP.

(30) a. *ani ma'arix* [$_{S}$ *še-hu yikne* ***et ha-sefer***]
I estimate that-he will-buy **OM the-book**

b. ***et ha-sefer*** *ani ma'arix* [$_{S}$ *še-hu yikne*]
OM the-book I estimate that-he will-buy

c. ****ani ma'arix meod*** [$_{S}$ *še-hu yikne et ha-sefer*]
I estimate very-much that-he will-buy OM the-book

(31) a. *ani ma'arix et* [$_{NP}$ *ze* [$_{S}$ *še-hu yikne* **et ha-sefer**]]
I appreciate OM it that-he will-buy OM the-book

b. ****et ha-sefer*** *ani ma'arix et* [$_{NP}$ *ze* [$_{S}$ *še-hu yikne*]]
OM the-book I appreciate OM it that-he will-buy

c. *ani ma'arix meod et* [$_{NP}$ *ze* [$_{S}$ *še-hu yikne et ha-sefer*]]
I appreciate very-much OM it that-he will-buy the-book

In (30) the node immediately following the V is S. One observes that PPP can apply to such structures (cf. the grammaticality of (30) b) but on the other hand the morpheme *meod* 'very much' renders the structure ungrammatical, as in (30) c. However in (31), where the hypothesized constituent structure is V [P [NP [S]]], the distributional facts of (31) b and c are the exact opposite of their counterparts in (30) b and (30) c: PPP is blocked in (31) b whereas *meod* is allowed (31) c.

The difference in grammaticality judgements between (30) b and (31) b is accounted for syntactically in terms of the NPC: the application of PPP must be blocked where it has the effect of moving elements out of an S embedded in a NP. The difference between (30) c and (31) c can also be accounted for syntactically once a distinction is made between PP complements and S complements: *meod* will be subcategorized as occurring only with verbs that take PP as complements.

3.2 *The various syntactic features of* le-ha'arix *and their semantic correlates*

With regard to considerations of meaning, one observes that the verb has different meaning in the different structures. The interpretation of (30) a is 'I guess/estimate that he will buy the book' whereas (31) a is interpreted as 'I appreciate the fact that he will buy the book'. It seems, then, that there is a correlation between the interpretation given to the verb *le-ha'arix*, the morphemes that can cooccur with it and the applicability of movement rules to the embedded sentences that follow the verb. All these facts can properly be accounted for if the verb *le-ha'arix* is subcategorized as occurring in the context of either an S or a PP. When in the context S, movement rules that move elements out of an embedded S can apply but *meod* cannot occur. On the other hand, when in the context PP, i.e. when the embedded S is dominated by a NP, movement rules cannot apply but *meod* can occur. One possible reason for the nonoccurrence of *meod* 'very' with the meaning 'guess/estimate' may stem from the fact that an adverb of degree cannot cooccur with verbs indicating uncertainty. This observation is supported by verbs such as *maniax* 'assume', *mešaer* 'suppose', etc. which are followed by S only and do not admit *meod* either.

(32) **hu maniax meod še-hem ayefim*
He assumes much that-they tired

(33) **hu mešaer meod še-hem ayefim*[6]
He supposed much that-they tired

Another example to support this claim made above is found in the use of *le-havin* 'to gather/understand'. In this case the difference in meaning is not as apparent as in (30) and (31). However, there is a definite difference which can be understood if we question the truth of the embedded S or deny its content.

(34) a. *ani mevina* [$_S$ *še-karter zaxa* ***ba-bexirot***]
I gather that-Carter won **in-the-elections**

b. ***ba-bexirot*** *ani mevina* [$_S$ *še-karter zaxa*]
In-the-elections I gather that-Carter won

c. *ani mevina* [$_S$ *še-karter zaxa ba-bexirot*] . *haim ze be-emet naxon?*
I gather that-Carter won in-the-elections. QUESTION it really true?

[6]This has been pointed out to me by Hetzron (personal communication).

(35) a. *ani mevina* [$_{PP}$ *et* [$_{NP}$ *ze* [$_{S}$ *še-karter zaxa* ***ba-bexirot***]]]
I understand OM it that-Carter won **in-the-elections**

b. ****ba-bexirot*** *ani mevina* [$_{PP}$ *et* [$_{NP}$ *ze* [$_{S}$ *še-karter zaxa*]]]
In-the-elections I understand OM it that-Carter won

c. **ani mevina* [$_{PP}$ *et* [$_{NP}$ *ze* [$_{S}$ *se-karter zaxa ba-bexirot*]]] . *haim ze be-emet naxon?*
I understand OM it that-Carter won in-the-elections. QUESTION it really true?

d. *ani mevina* [$_{PP}$ *et* [$_{NP}$ *ze* [$_{S}$ *še-karter zaxa ba-bexirot*]]] , *aval ani lo meruce mi-ze*
I understand OM it that-Carter won in-the-elections, but I am not satisfied from it

In (34) the verb is followed by an S and therefore movement out of the embedded S is allowed as in b. In addition, since the S which follows the verb is not necessarily believed to be true by the structure of the sentence, it is possible to ask whether the content of the embedded S is true or not as in c. The meaning of the verb in all three cases is approximately 'to gather'.

In (35) where the V is followed by a PP, the meaning of the verb is 'to understand'. In these cases movement rules cannot apply since their application will constitute a violation of the NPC as in b. As for the questioning of the truth of the embedded S, this is also impossible since the truth of the embedded clause is assumed by the structure as in c (Kiparsky and Kiparsky 1971).

Again it seems that the correlation between the meaning of the verb, the syntactic behavior of the sentences with respect to movement rules, and the cooccurrence restrictions is not accidental. I suggest that all of these facts can be captured by a proper subcategorization of the verbs and if the constituent NP is given semantic content as explained in Section 4.

4. A Semantic Analysis

4.1 *Subcategorization of verbs allowing sentential complements*

It has been shown in the preceding discussion that in order to account for various grammaticality judgements it was necessary to distinguish between two categories of embedded sentences: S's dominated by a NP (NP–S) and S's not so dominated. Accordingly, the verbs under consideration have been subcategorized as occurring either with an NP–S, an S not dominated by a NP, or both. These verbs, then, are classified as follows. (No distinction is made here with respect to the tense or the conjugations of the verbal elements. All forms are given in III person masculine singular.)

(36) **NP–S**		(37) **S**	
sameax (al)	'happy (about)'	*mešaer*	'hypothesize'
acuv (al)	'sad (about)'	*mavtiax*	'promise'
micta'er (al)	'sorry (about)'	*mekave*	'hope'
meucban (al)	'nervous (about)'	*savur*	'be of the opinion'
mecuvrax (al)	'moody'	*maniax*	'assume'

meyuaš (me)	'despair'	*nidme l-*	'seems to'
mešune	'strange' (impersonal)	*dome*	'seems' (impersonal)
adiš	'indifferent'	*nire l-*	'seems to'
meyaxel	'expect anxiously'	*yitaxen*	'may be'
		yaxol lihyot	'be possible'

(38) **NP–S**

ciyen (et)	'praise' 'mention'
niba (et)	'predict' 'guess'
mecape (le)	'expect anxiously' 'expect'
maarix (et)	'appreciate' 'estimate'
mevin (et)	'understand' 'figure'
maxriz (be-, al)	'declare' 'announce'
mitrašem (mi)	'think' 'be impressed by'
modia (al)	'report (about)'
yodea (al)	'know (about)'
šomea (al)	'hear (about)'
medaveax (al)	'report (about)'
xošev (al)	'think (about)' [7]

The group of verbs in (36, NP–S) is the same as factive verbs described by Kiparsky and Kiparsky (1971: 345-360); the second group (37, S) corresponds to their nonfactive class. Kiparsky and Kiparsky claim that the distinction between factive and nonfactive verbs is that with the factive "the speaker presupposes that the embedded clause expresses a true proposition and makes some assertion about that proposition" (1971: 348). In the case of the nonfactive verbs the embedded S is not a presupposition of the entire S but rather part of what the entire S asserts. The different structures that Kiparsky and Kiparsky assign to the two types of verbs is given in (39).

(39)

FACTIVE NON-FACTIVE

---

[7] The difference in meaning in verbs such as *modia, yodea, somea,* etc. is a question of degree of certainty. This difference is best illustrated when the embedded S is fronted and differences of acceptability emerge.

e.g. (i) a. *moše lo šama* [$_S$ *še-hem mitgaršim*]
Moses not heard that-they are-getting-a-divorce

b. *[$_S$ *še-hem mitgaršim*] *mose lo sama*
That-they are-getting-a-divorce Moses not heard

(ii) a. *mose lo šama* [$_{PP}$ *al* [$_{NP}$ *ze* [$_S$ *še-hem mitgaršim*]
Moses not heard about it that-they are-getting-a-divorce

b. [$_{PP}$ *al* [$_{NP}$ *ze* [$_S$ *še-hem mitgaršim*] *moše lo šama*
About it that-they are-getting-a-divorce Moses not heard

For similar examples and a more comprehensive discussion cf. Hooper and Thompson (1973).

If we were to adapt the Kiparskys' framework to the data presented here, we would have to classify verbs as being either [+FACTIVE] (36) or [−FACTIVE] (37) or [±FACTIVE] (38). Such an analysis would make the claim that the difference in meaning between the two types of verbs is attributed to the arbitrary node *fact* in (39).

One disadvantage of such an analysis is that it cannot account in a simple way for the syntactic facts of Hebrew. As was demonstrated earlier (18-20), there are S's following verbs of the [+FACTIVE] group which despite their not being preceded by a head NP have to be dominated by a NP. (These embedded S's, one may recall, are all subject to the NPC.)[8] If the [−FACTIVE] verbs are derived from a deep structure similar to (39), there is no way of explaining the syntactic facts accounted for in the present analysis, i.e. there is no way of capturing the difference in the syntactic behavior of an NP–S and an S not dominated by a NP.

4.2 *Syntactic nodes as meaning contributors*

Let us now turn to a discussion of a possible semantic explanation. The discussion is based on two general premises (a, b below) and two specific distinctions (c, d below).

(a) The postulation of a syntactic structure has to be relevant to the semantic interpretation as well as to the syntactic analysis.[9]

(b) Homonomy is an empirical question; it should be postulated only as the last option for distinguishing between various readings of a morpheme.

(c) Hebrew requires a distinction between V–[NP–S] and [V–S] and verbs are subcategorized accordingly.

(d) Some embedded S's are presuppositions of the sentence in which they are embedded and some are not. An NP–S is a presupposition, i.e. it has truth value. As such the embedded S expresses either an event or a state that exists, or has reference independently of the entire S.[10] On the other hand an S which is not dominated by a NP does not have such an independent existence.[11]

---

[8]Thus far I am not aware of an adequate rule that can delete the node *fact* if we were to assume such an analysis for the SNP verbs.

[9]See Perlmutter (1970) for an implicit similar approach to the relation between the readings of verbs and their syntactic subcategorization.

[10]Cf. Kiparsky and Kiparsky (1971: 366(I)) where a correspondence is noted between *truth* and specific reference.

[11]Two examples illustrating the above observations are

(i) *dan* *sameax* $[_{NP}$ $[_{S}$ *še-moše* *ba*]
Dan happy that-Moses came

The fact that Moses came is independent of the fact that Dan is happy about it. However, in

(ii) *dan* *meša'er* $[_{S}$ *še-moše* *ba*]
Dan assumes that-Moses came

the embedded S *še-moše ba* does not express a fact at all.

Examining the structure where a NP–S appears, e.g. (22-24), (31),one observes that the verb that can cooccur with it is one whose meaning is such that it *does* or *can be perceived* as asserting something about an event or a state. Thus, for example, one can be *sameax* 'happy', *acuv* 'sad', *me'ucban* 'nervous', or *adiš* 'indifferent' about a particular event. On the other hand, in cases where S appears, e.g. (16-17), (30), one finds verbs that express either a desire for a particular event or state to occur, as for example *mitxanen* 'beg/implore', or other verbs that express uncertainty about whether a particular event or state really exists, as for example *maniax* 'hypothesize', *mešaʼer* 'assume', etc.

The difference between the interpretations given to these two types of verb could in principle be accounted for as part of the differences in the meanings of these verbs, i.e. assign the verb a feature which requires a presupposition to follow in one case and restrict such a presupposition in the other. But given the correlation between the type of verbs and the behavior of the structures they occur in, it is possible that the semantic facts are not to be attributed to the meaning of the verbs but rather to the meaning of the structures. That is, NP–S has a meaning or makes a contribution to the interpretation of the entire S which is not made by an S not so dominated. In particular, the fact that the content of the embedded S is presupposed allows for, or even requires, that there be a comment on the content of this S. Therefore the verb is interpreted in such a context, as adding a comment.[12] Such a feature of meaning cannot be present when the embedded S is not dominated by a NP.

The different interpretations assigned to verbs such as *le-ha'arix* 'to estimate' 'to appreciate' can thus be explained, partially at least, in the following way. The verb *le-ha'arix* can be followed by either a NP or an S.[13] When followed by a NP dominating an S, the S must be interpreted as an existing situation on which the main verb must comment, if it is to contribute anything to the meaning of the utterance. In other words, the verb cannot simply assert the event in the embedded sentence because its existence is already expressed by the fact that the S is dominated by a NP. This is exactly what is added to the meaning of the verb *le-ha'arix* when it has the meaning of 'to appreciate'—a value judgement on an existing situation. No such value judgement is found when the S following the verb is not dominated by a NP since before a judgement can be made on a situation, the situation has to exist.

The extent to which the structure contributes to the meaning extends from being redundant to being crucial as explained in the following examples:

(40) a. *ani mictaer* [$_{NP}$ [$_S$ *še-lo higatem*]]
I sorry that-not you-arrived

b. *ani mictaer* [$_{PP}$ *al* [$_{NP}$ [$_S$ *še-lo-higatem*]]]
I sorry about that-not you-arrived

c. *ani mictaer* [$_{PP}$ *al* [$_{NP}$ *ze* [$_S$ *še-lo higatem*]]]
I sorry about it that-not you-arrived

[12]It should be noted that the meaning 'comment' is only one feature of the meaning and that there are other factors which determine the ultimate interpretation.

[13]Rubinstein (1971: 73-90) makes similar observations. However he does not show the possible connections between the change in meaning and the structure.

The interpretation of all three sentences is 'I am sorry that you have not arrived'. The verb *le-hictaer* 'to be sorry' should include as part of its meaning the feature [+ comment] because its meaning in all contexts involves a value judgement. Given this feature of the verb, it is clear that the node NP which dominated the embedded S is redundant. In the same way the head NP and the Prep. which indicate that what follows is dominated by a NP are also redundant and therefore can be absent from the structure without changing the meaning.

(41) a. *ani mexaka* [$_S$ *še-hem yagiu*]
I wait that-they will-arrive

b. **ani mexaka* [$_S$ *le še-hem yagiu*]
I wait for that-they will-arrive

c. *ani mexaka* [$_{PP}$ *la-* [$_{NP}$ *ze* [$_S$ *še-hem yagiu*]]]
I wait for-it that-they will-come

The meaning of (41) a is 'I am waiting till they arrive' where no commitment is made by the speaker as to whether they will arrive or not and therefore no value judgement is present. In (41) c however, the meaning is 'I am expecting them to arrive'. It is clear from the structure that they are coming and therefore the added value judgement. The verb *le-xakot* is different from *le-hictaer* in that it does not include a comment but rather describes an objective state. In order to get a meaning of *le-xakot* which does include the 'expectation', the S which follows the verb must be embedded in a NP. The *le-ze* 'for-it' are therefore the indications that there is a NP which follows. Given that the verb does not include the feature [+ expectation], the [Prep. + *ze*] are obligatory.

We turn now to sentences (1-4), which are repeated below for clarity, to provide an explanation for the various readings associated with the verb in each one of them.

(1) *ani meta še-yatxilu kvar tiyulim le-kahir*
'I would very much like to see that trips to Cairo would already begin'

(2) *ani meta al ha-sefer ha-ze*
'I am crazy about this book'

(3) *ani meta al ha-raayon še-nisa le-kahir*
'I am crazy about the idea that we will travel to Cairo'

(4) *ani meta al ha-raayon še-hicata*
'I am crazy about the idea that you have proposed'

The verb *la-mut* 'to die' in isolation does not include any comment. It is categorized as ________PP where the PP is either causal or instrumental. For example, *la-mut mi-maxala* 'to die of disease', *la-mut mi-caar* 'to die of grief'. One should notice that the Prep. *mi-* 'from/of' in this context cannot be followed by a sentential complement of N as the ungrammaticality of (42) indicates.

(42) **hu met mi-ze se-ha-rofe lo higia ba-zman*
He died of-it that-the-doctor not arrived in-time

It seems that the change which occurs with the verb *la-mut* is that it allows for a node S to follow it immediately. Given the regularity explained above, it is predictable that the interpretation of *la-mut*, whatever its new reading may be, cannot include a comment if the S which follows is not dominated by a NP, i.e. we get the meaning 'want'. On the other hand once the preposition *al* 'about' replaces *mi-* 'from/of' and allows for an embedded NP–S to follow, this NP node requires that the verb includes a comment and we get the meaning 'love' (1-4).

A question which is left unanswered in this paper is why *la-mut* gets the meaning of 'want' or 'love'. However, it seems clear that in creating new forms of expression in the language, the novelty is only partial; new forms use some regularity that already exists in the language and which is still productive.

REFERENCES

Ben Horin, Gad. 1976. "Aspects of syntactic preposing in spoken Hebrew." In Cole (1976), pp. 193-208.

Berman, Ruth. 1976. "On derived and deriving nominals in Hebrew." In Cole (1976), pp. 57-98.

Chayen, M. J. and Z. Dror. 1976. *Introduction to Hebrew Transformational Grammar.* Israel, University Publishing Projects Ltd.

Cole, Peter. 1976. *Studies in Modern Hebrew Syntax and Semantics.* Amsterdam: North Holland.

Hooper, Joan B. and Sandra A. Thompson. 1973. "On the applicability of root transformations." **Linguistic Inquiry** 4: 465-97.

Jackendorff, Ray S. 1972. *Semantic Interpretation in Generative Grammar.* Cambridge, Mass.: M.I.T. Press.

Katz, Jerrold J. and Paul Postal. 1964. *An Integrated Theory of Linguistic Description.* Cambridge, Mass.: M.I.T. Press.

Kiparsky, Paul and Carol Kiparsky. 1971. "Fact." In Steinberg and Jacobovitz (1971), pp. 345-369.

Klima, Edward S. 1964. "Negation in English." In J. A. Fodor and J. J. Katz (eds.), *The Structure of Language,* pp. 246-323. Englewood Cliffs, N.J.: Prentice-Hall.

Lakoff, George. 1971. "On generative semantics." In Steinberg and Jacobovitz (1971), pp. 232-296.

Perlmutter, David M. 1970. "The two verbs begin." In R. A. Jacobs and P. S. Rosenbaum (eds.), *Readings in English Transformational Grammar,* pp. 107-119. Waltham, Mass.: Xerox Publishing Co.

Rosenbaum, Peter S. 1967. *The Grammar of English Predicate Complement Structure.* Cambridge, Mass.: M.I.T. Press.

Ross, J. 1967. *Constraints of Variables in Syntax.* Doctoral dissertation, M.I.T. [Reproduced 1968 by Indiana University Linguistics Club.]

Rubinstein, E. 1971. *The Verb Phrase.* Israel: Hakibbutz Hameuchad.

Steinberg, Danny D. and Leon A. Jacobovitz, eds. 1971. *Semantics.* Cambridge: Cambridge University Press.